The American Couple

The American Couple

Jayasri Gill

To order additional copies of this book, contact:
Xlibris Corporation
1-888-795-4274
www.Xlibris.com
Orders@Xlibris.com
94769

Contents

Introduction I

PUNAM DID NOT realize that her only house is already broken into pieces. She just wake up in the mid of the night and her alarm clock is an hour away to put her onto the next day.

No, this can't be happening! There is a Father in the heaven who takes care of me. I can't be left alone in the dark. My water in boiling for two coffee cups. My knees are rigid to move on. Dear God, how in the blasphemy land, I had to lose everything? – e-v-e-r-y t-h-i-n-g?

The days routines are fixed for Punam and her only life partner, Bibi. They crunched together for five little years now. The web and tide went through but, could not loosen the tie. Every morning is a morning. It is up to Punam to make two cups of coffee to break the day.

Bibi is always late. For Bibi, the warm cup of coffee sings like a bird. He cherishes it so much. Bibi can't realize, how long they are sharing a life together. In Bibis mind, they are always there together since they were born.

The idleness and the fear of losing their only apartment became real to both of them now. It can't be prolonged any further. They already did there recurring mistakes. Mistakes? – no it's a deep deep drawback in habituating the American life. Both of them did the same recurring slam dung – Big mistakes again, they trusted their poorly neighbors. Help the neighbors like your own brothers – did not work out well.

All of their savings are gone, the jobs are sliding on a single string and the chaos formed pretty easily on and after their credit histories.

Rushing for anything won't work more now.

The chantalising big fat hollow is embracing Punam all through. Her mind says STOP!, period. But, the dark fat hollow is comming up to take out all the prides and the roof on the head for the twos.

The alarm is ringing high. She stood up straight and had all the fears gone. It is a battle field to take care. Her mind started boggling over and over again. Where to go next, what to eat, how to get ready for the slim – job in hands??

Punam tried to rationalize her action again. As the head of the house, she has to make all quick decisions and the next thing is to carry these over. She looked up at Bibi. Bibis eyes are pale blue. He has hazel eyes but, now his eyes are pale blue. The very last thing Punam could remember is that they were both awake and were waiting for a knife to slide thorough from Mr. Monster. He was just hovering in outside. They could hear the noise of his gasps.

Nothing happened since then. Both of them fall asleep at some points in the big dark night. All the door vails are unhurt, as well as are the walls of the apartment house. Hearing deeply for the footsteps in outside, she could not hear anything distinguishing and fearing. But, Bibi is not in a mood this morning. His eyes are still pale blue – not green, not hazel, as is normal for him.

Bibi, Bibi, wake up now. This is morning again. Nothing to fear any more. We can call for the police and we have not sit tight for the Monster's knife. Our bed is still one piece and the same are the vails at the doors. You can also watch the kitchen, nothing is broke and the coffee water is ready!

Bibi now started sobbing poorly. Ohoh, ohoh. Nobody here will care for us now. Is there a God, who can care for us two as well? Nothing will stop us from being out of roof and being all at the Monsters. If you know of the size of his foot step, you can't ignore me, ignore my fear any more. Do you think that Autria police will come and save us from the Muster? They are all lined up to him and his colleagues. You call them, they will rob you off further and can perish us both as well. Oh my gosh, why we came here? Why you could not figure it out that Mr. Monster was here and now we are all gone!! It is all your fault, nobody else's!! . . . .

Get ready

THE WATER LEVEL is rising. One, two, three, Four . . . . I am gone, bye Pun! . . . Hah, Hah, Hah, Hah!!

I am gone Bibi!! . . . .

Don't Don't. Ahhhh!!! You can't! Listen to Me, do not just Joke, Okaay!!. Hold my hand and we jump out together. And, if you go, I will go too. Remember, Do not joke!!! . . . .

Ready, One, Two, Three!! We are floating now Bibi!!! . . . .

My Gosh, We could make it!!!, Ahahhh!!!!! . . . .

Here we go again!! One, two, three, four, five. Let's step up further, Okay!!! . . . .

Ready, hold hands tight, here we go!! . . . .

Rrarr, Rarrrr, Rarrr, rrrr, rrrrr . . . . Bibi, we are there!! We are the Surfer now!! . . . .

Well, I knew that you could do it too. Just a little patience, well?!!.

Rarrrrr, Rarrrr, Rarrr, Whuhoh!!!! . . . .

Bibi, we really made it. I feel like riding here again and again. I won't go back to the motel! . . . .

Well, we have some time in hands. But, I am kind of a little tired. It's your turn now, to hold my hands and balance me . . .

Ready, One, two, three, four Rururrrr, Rururrrrrrrrrrr . . . . Bibi, I can't ahhhhh!! . . . . Tightened now . . . Just stay back at your feet . . . ohuh, ohuh, oach!! . . . . All sands and funjis around me . . . Do I smell now?! . . . I am going home . . .

Well, I got tired too and is smelling is n't it? . . .

Let's go home, we are all done for today!! Will come back tomorrow, if you want!! I am hungry and tired!!! . . . My feet are all hurting now and hands too. How are yours?!!

Mine are tired too, but I think, you took the pressure mostly. So I am tired and smelly too but, not very hungry!! . . .

Anyway, let's go home for today!! Is there anyway to take off these dirty sands.? My feet are hurting bad too.

There is a shower for Guys and Girls at the shore and we can wash up and can were sandals before going to the car. How did you like it?

Bibi, I liked it very much, though I needed to wash us up before sitting in the car. I liked the waves so much. You get light and lighter further when you ride; it it so much amazing!! I like to stay here for a while. It is hot now at the Sun, at noon. I though love the hot, warmness. I liked the scaly smell too, I think!!

You are just a Girl, not a mature Bau !! . . . I am basically older to you!! Also that I holded ourselves up!! Hold me wrapped now!!

Bibi, you are still an American! I don't feel like doing that in front of the eyes. Are you mad? All the guys and Girls are holding themselves together!! It is not India, for sure!! . . . I just like it in that way!! . . . You have not to hold me, if you feel embarrassed here.

Back now in the tiny little home of ours. The rest of the day is all ours!! Do you mind if I will shower first? . . . .

Go ahead, I think I like your Scaly smell to on me. I rather watch the Basket Ball game now . . .

Just yell at me when you are done!!!

Bibi, I am clean, but the scaly smell is still there a little. It's you r turn!! . . . . Hurrah!!! . . .

Coby is dodging, ohah, he got it . . . I will be just back!! . . . Wait for me before you do make any food!!

There it is a little cat at the door. I rather keep the door open, until you come back!! Do not take too long to wash yourself now! . . . .

On the Moon ride, in the cool night, I want to be there, in the hot summer, in the top corner, I wanna to be there.

Bibi, I do not want to be better than that. This is such a cool beach and the weather is so gorgeous. Can we buy a house out here and stay forever?!!

I knew, that I will hear something like that!! . . . How, did you read my mind Bibi?!!

I do not know, how I do so, but – I literally read your mind, even before you say the word, I knew what you are up to. This is God, I think that I got it straight and I can get my life full!! This is the greatest thing that has ever happened to me and I can just carry you around anywhere and in my life. Look what I got, Ahahahh . . . . !!

Bibi, do not boast so much, people are not that all are so good. Who knows what can happen to us!! Sometimes I feel so sad that my parents are there in the other part of the globe and look at us, we are married and warm up here. I am not sad, but is curious enough to get to know the truth.

The Mavin beach

MAVIN BEACH IS cool and also that I like to be here around. But, my money is all going away from the severance pay. When will you get your Green card citizenship and can work again? Is it the same immigration system in India too? I wonder, why you came here, instead – I could have gone there and got the Indian green card citizenship!!

Bibi, some times, I feel so lucky that I got you and got married to you too. I do not think, all the people are so lucky really. Especially when I think of my friends, I do not think that they always chose the right person – the man or the woman that they liked. I think, I like America with this freedom of choice. It is so cool here. And there is no Indian Green card system, it's a direct citizenship when you marry someone. I hardly knew that there is such an immigration system in America!! I hardly could realize that I had to have a mandatory waiting period for working again. This is all such a bull – shit!!

Punam and Bibi stayed in Mavin beach for a while now and watched the gorgeous sunrise and sunset everyday in the dawn and in the dusk. But, time ran away and they had to pack back to return to Fairview – a little bit away from their honeymoon beach, where Bibi got a job from the local work force center, next to it. They are still happy and the money could never ran away.

The days started good all in its shape. In the morning, it is Bibi's duty to wake Punam up and make ready to have the breakfast done. With the opening of eyes, it is always a fresh new day for Punam. She is ready to have the break fast ready in just a little bit and warms up the Nissan Altima for the days journey, for dropping

Bibi to the work. Punam has her whole day to shine on the Art job while being out of work.

Punam is busy in polishing the new water color portrait of Oceanic view, just a little picture of her mind, of the Helosinki beach. The Phone rang once, twice, thrice and hello, this is Punam here. Hah, hah, hah, wanted to get you a surprise in the day. I came out of work and I can't eat these things at the Coral star, next to my work. You thought of that you can get away so easily – just by dropping me off!! I can imagine, how I would feel like, if I have to do the same for you.

You need to bring me something that you got. I need to eat properly to make money.

Well Bibi, no hurry. I will just be there. I did not cook yet but, can get something to eat with you there. I will be there in ten minutes.

Punam rushed away to their family work site while Bibi is waiting at the table after ordering a glass of skimmed milk. The couple shared their lunch and Punam promised to get back, ten minutes before 5'o clock.

The cove

PUNAM IS READY to drop Bibi off at the work and is planning to make errands to take care of the couple's mortgage and other credit bills. With the lower level income, it is always tight to handle the bills better. Punam is frustrated the way United states immigration works. In her mind, it should have been as straight as it works in different other countries, including her own country India. She feels she is betrayed up here alone and the immigration lawyer is purely bogus, to kill all the five months now – at this low joint income level, which is just Bibis income. Her only contribution is to make Bibi ready for the work, drop him there, eat lunch and get back to home after work. It is good to be married and have a joint life, but the money is so little to manage the whole household. Sometimes she gets frustrated at her – she feels something better that she could have done rather to bit this U.S. immigration process, it's prolonged processing scheme – even after marrying a citizen here.

All her school days were that cool as well as were her previous work. She was working fine at her previous job until the circus has changed her way to think of the U.S. work place.

The Circus, what about it – what happened? Bibi promised to take the whole incident off of her mind until the couple could take a step further. Bibi is very cool with his mindset. Nothing bothers him as long as he can get back to Punam, after work. They like to watch TV, the basket ball game specially at ESPV or watch some NetClip movies of choice.

The circus I

THE CIRCUS IS still there in Punams mind, especially when alone at the home – while Bibi is at work. Punam tried to research the matter on the internet several times. In her online research, she never found anything as 'Anomaly pass' as happened at the interiew in Dorn City, Tx when she was looking for her second job in America. She already left her first job as a junior art manager while she had the better job offer from her client company or its subsidiaries. SubnetMask is a multinational company in the art industry in the central part of North America. So its clientle list is big too with the supply – chain-management. Nobody ever got harassed by the local laws – just for taking an interview with some clientale chain conducted at the same premises, after quiting the company. This issue will remain in her head like a headche, though Bibi promised to – not to think about it anytime and he is going to take care of it.

Bibi has an extra day in this weekend. It is Thanks giving day, before the Saturday. Punam prepared their dual meal nicely. The dinner table is ready with four pieces of Indian Chapati, an oven roasted turkey with pickes and seasonings of Drobson Brothers. It smells good really and Bibi is a great fan of Chapati bread. They enjoyed the dinner in gloomy light inside of the house.

Bibi is so relaxed that he has a total extra day for lavish spending with Punam. These days are kind of rare. After dinner, his plan is to go for a movie, probably any Silverstar Stalone or Star Track voyeger. Punam likes his choice of movie selection or any brand music selection. She still has the whole plate in front of her to get used to. Bibi feels he the the luckiest man to be here. Nothing was planned before, but that it just happened and worked so well. Bibi does not bother if somebody else makes more money or that they could have better food and drink.

Bibi was born in America but, he wants to go whereever Punam would feel to go. They have the house now and if things would change, they can sell it may be, or get another house somewhere else. Bibi knows that Punam likes the proper cities better. In her upbringing, she likes a society culture better than having fun and relaxing atmosphere. Bibi's thought broke when the phone rang after dinner.

The circus2

WHO CALLED AT this time – do not they know that today is Thanks giving dinner. It may be his parents, who are wishing him and his family.

Hi Ricky – this is Halinda here from your work. I thought of giving you asurprise after Thanks giving dinner. What you people eat today?

– Ohah my Gosh, I never meant to be that popular to her or to anybody – to discuss our menus. It was all my day otherwise, rather than the 'Butter Fingers' . . . . Ohah, we just finished eating. It was some thing very simple – some Indian bread and some Turky – that's it. How was yours? Oahahhhhhah, we are not American Christians. We all eat different delicious plates – that you cann't imagine. Do you like to join us someday, how about tomorrow? . . . .

No, we will be busy tomorrow, but may be someday, I can taste your food. Thanks a lot!! Blunk!! . . . .

Uhah, she does not know that today was Thanks Giving!! – She has put forward her menus that I could like now!! How do you think that I feel – after consuming our dinner of the day – at the table? Can you please explain me what the culture is there in India – specially after some celebrating day!! She is so much uncurtesious that she even forgot to make it for upto two.

Punam baffled on the conversation of the two but, could not have a better explanation than Bibis – what is the Indian culture with the neighbours after a celebrating day, specially when they are two separate famiies or groups of friends. This elderly woman works in that office as a HR clerk and is not of Punam' s any circle – to say about her. As is the AMerican culture, this woman is a gladder of some men working in Rocker's place – Punam could hardly think of anything better. It is better to be silent, rather than saying anything into it.

Melancholy Marvelous

PUNAM IS READY to pick Bibi up after the errands are all done for the day and is heading for the Rocker's place, where Bibi has his new work. Mr. Donald is Bibi's boss, the owner of Rocker's place. He is the nephew of the actual owner of the company, Punam forgot his name; she hardly has seen him, even though she goes to the reception each and everyday.

Punam is honking now, to make sure that Bibi hears it clearly – that she is already here. For God's sake, why Bibi is getting late today? Did they give him some miscelleneous task to complete – what they never appreciate of or compensate for Bibi? BEEP, Beep!! Bibi is still not there now! Is there anything, that could have happened, my God! Is Bibi alright? Som epanic is grasping on the face of Punam. A cold wave nerved her out. She is still waiting at the parking lot, waiting to pick Bibi up. All her shoppings are laying down on the back seat. It is the winter time, but she strated feeling Hot and warm – for no other reason.

Noh, there is no sign of Bibi. Normally before he could hear a beap, he comes out – to present him more vigorant and active to Punam. It is always there as long as they are there together and since when they met. Punam is wondering if his boss has sent Bibi out to anywhere for the business sake. So closed the drivers door of their Altima and came out straight to the office door, next to the Workforce center branch in west California.

Hello and good afternoon. Can I talk to Bibi, is he not done yet please? . . . . Hum . . . Can I get your name please, asked the olderly reception lady at the desk of Rocker's place. Punam has seen this lady a few times only walking around the small corridors in the work place office. She knew that all this clearks and reception people knew her well enough to tell about Bibi, as they knew them as the husband and wife for a long time now.

Yes, this is Punam, Bibi's wife. Can you please call for him, we are already late for today afternoon?

No, wait. You do not have the permmission to go inside and I cann't call Bibi. I do not know if he is your husband or not. Please do not ask me anything else and excuse me now!

Shut, what is happening! Punam cann't trust her eyes and ears. Are they playing any kind of joke! But, the lady has a stiff face – which is not a joke, for sure. Ms Anglica or what – is about sixty years old and was never be this much desperate beforfe. Punam know for certain that she is in the trouble and she has no one else of her own to tell her anything further. She felt like falling down to her knee; somehow she managed herself to come out of the office cabin and the cold air wrapped her around. The next door workforce center is now closed adn it is dark in the outside now. Punam hurried up to the car and rested for a while before starting the enigine. She honked again for the final time, incase it is all made up and nothing happened wrong!!. Noh, God may have closed his eyes on her. She has to make any sense out of it. Punam is driving towards their home and looking around the street incase, Bibi started walking back – if he got off early and Punam came late than may be for a four – thirty closure for Bibi!! All the street light are so meticulous on both sides of the street and people are gathering around on laughing faces – young and old, but no one is Bibi.

The Ugly Odds

O AH MY GOD – CAN you tell me what can I do now? Is it common for America that somebody can just go missing all of a sudden? Teh hard black fear is springing into her vein slowly and still there is no sign of Bibi – a lad of twenty five years old – six feet two inches tall in white – red skin, caucassian with the hazle – green eyes came out from the work place or from anywhere on the road. The lights, sirens of passing cars, roadside bands, a few couples adn men and women passed by with no trace of Bibi. Punam unlatched the door and sat flat – sobbing silently loosening her neck at the sofa – table.

Wait one, two, three and count upto ten. What sense it makes now? My lights are all on and the outside road is dark but the street lights are on and bright. It's not any kind of a mistake that Bibi is in a trouble for sure. Is he alive or dead by this time! What is the tiem now. Ten minutes past seven. She was there for at least two hours at the Rocker's or around at the streets. She is sweating and is actually nervous. How can she cope up with this by herself single handedly now? The home has a neat fireplace for their relaxation and she chose to be there at the fireplace to embrace her fear. She got up and shoallowed a glass of warm water kept at the table for their afternoon tea. It tastes bitter too. May be that she got upset for some reason and is feverish – so nothing wrong has happened to Bibi and it is just the timing that went wrong! May be that in her own stiff head, she is seeing all mess. It may be something else – what she cann't figure out now. She put on the gas heater to make some tea to herself and started the TV with the news channel on.

This is ABC news broad casting the evening news on Tuesday, May, 2001. Good evening. This is partly cloudy sky with temperature 45 degrees. The hot news for today is that a water tank broke up at the Rodendo beach area about this afternoon; nobody is injured and the workers of the water department is still repairing the tank . . . The police raided a cargo van running at the sixteenth street with the back tank of the car open. The news of the spot light is that the Lakers lost today to yankies on 32 to 50. There is some slight snow possible in the night. No major accident or injury on the roads . . . .

Punam shut down the Tv and started counting upto hundred at the wall. tears broke out of her eyes now. She is feeling a solid pain sliding through her veins. She sipped tea again and got up and called 911 . . .

Hello, this is Punam here at 1317 Wanderhollow street. My husband seems to be missing from his work at the Rockers in Midtown district . . . Mam, slow it down! What happened, your husband went missing today? How do you think that he did not go to somewhere after his work? How old he is? – Twenty five years old white guy, a senior artist at the Rockers? Okay calm down, let us send some officer there who can take down the report. He may not be missing at all, he may have gone to somewhere else . . . It is not likely that an adult goes missing all of a sudden, specially from the work.

The Play

RING, RING, RING. Punam opened her doors apart. Two policemans are there looking around the whole area of her lobby and all. What is your name mam? – what is your husband's name? How much is his weight, height, color – white!! How long he is working at the Rocker's? Is he seeing someone else that you could tell? – no, well, we think that is what has happended to him. You cannot say that he is missing unless he comes back within a few days. May be that he got tired of you and he chose to do something different. No, okay we will look around to see if he could be missing at all. What are hsi relatives and family members? They are not here, okay – here is your ticket number, and call us back if he returns. Good evening and take some rest for yourself! Shut . . . what they are thinking that I made something up and Bibi went to see somebody else, being bored at me!! . . . . Ohah my god, I would feel safe if that is the case!! . . .

The clock went on twelve, one, two, three, four, ... Punam fell asleep at her sofa. the next morning came up and still there is no sign of' Bibi – waiting or doing anything up here. Let's wait and wait to see what happened. Her head is now as rigid as is her sofa. She feels it could have been better if someone else could have been at her shoes, rather than her by herself. She got up and made herself a mug of coffee. She may got some ulser at the stomack by now, tha tis hurting bitterly. She cann't eat though, she may throw everything up. And she panicced and threw up everything from her stomack. A how shower could make her better!

She bathed and dressed up so that she is alive. She checked the news in the television – nothing is special! It again became night and she fell asleep and got up in the second morning by herself. No news from the police, no news at the teleision and there is no trace of Bibi. She now know for sure that her marriage is gone by now – either Bibi is alive or not. There is no phone call for her yet!

She got up and concentrated at her last drawing – a master piece of the bibliographic Christ – surrounding are the disciples – all are neat and clean adn are eager in their eyes to digest the doctrine alive! She strated hating the picture and thought of either to tear the pieces apart of it or to put some black ink pastle to make it more real in the world. The time went by, no phone call until it almost five o' clock on Thrusday.

Mimi, this is Bibi here. Are you okay? . . . Bibi's voice was something else like a strange old man's voice. Punam was not certain that it was Bibi really, though the strange voice was tired and stumbling at every stroke and that said that he is coming home in an hour from now! . . .

Punam was laughing at herself, crawling down on her knees on the floor with tears broke into her eyes. Bibi is still real and it should not be anything false!! Infact he is coming back home, so it has to be him – from anywhere!! . . . Also that all the conversation over the phone had a genuine tone of voice that only Bibi could have. Thanks to God, jesus and the biblical disciples that they are still alive at the holy grace. Just hold us up as we were and figure out the path that we could have from here, God, the mighty mercy!!

Venture1

BING, BING. PUNAM ran to the door with the hard, rigit knees again and clipped open the door knob. It is Bibi' statue, who is standing there. Punam toughed him on the veins at his right hand and it is him, real. She closed the door back and embraced him with his two arms. Bibi is something else. He has a very high fever, his face is all swolen and puffy and red; his hands and feets are shiering and he wanted to just hug her tight for moments. Punam thanked God and could not still hold herself back from the scaly smell that Bibi is releasing from his body; it looks like he could be just dying at her embracement itself. She loosened herself and ran for the basin at the bathroom. When she cam eback, Bibi's oldened body is resting flat on the floor and his body is hot in temperature. Punam tried to call the police, but the moment she got up, Bibi's body got up to hold her off from the phone. P-L-E-A-S-E, do not call the police, I am still okay!! Punam stopped and looked at him again and again – what happened to you, where you were, why you did not come out of your office – was I late??

No, no no. Just let me to rest here and Bibi took Punam's lap Teh hot ferent fever is coming out of his body and she has to do something to take care of his body now, otherwise he could be just gone right here. She took off his clothes and got some hot towel to wash his body off the smell and dirt and fatigue. Bibi laid there down tow days more at a stretch and could not get even to eat or drink. All punam could do is to swallow him some milk, berries and coffee until he gets better. She also got him some fever killer medicine to nurse him from there. The question remained in between – what happened, where and who did that?

Bibi cried out a few times that it was not him, sho did it but it was somebody else who used him to drag him down like that and he promised that he can be still well when Punam is there around. His oice was all gone strangely but, his moto was the same and simple. Punam could break through the scaly smell and can bear with the trouma patiently.

The Alpha

AFTER THREE TO five days, bibi wake up okay and could breath okay after the trouma has happened. Punam already made some curtesy call to the local police to let them know that Bib came back after two days and was totally ill. They did not bother about it and who knows what their report says!! The very strange feeling about being in America alomost knocked her down deeply. Who knows, how to make the stuffs right here! What should happen from here to us?? . . .

Bibi opened his mouth and told the inside details to Punma with a promise that 'you do not call police' – the promise rests on the fact that, 'if you call police, I obviously have no job, no immigration support from here for you'; also the threat is of international Mafia level. We cann't survive if either you or me go to the police or go for hospitalization assistance; the woman, who called me before on the Thnaks giving, raped me throughly after taking me off the work to her home. I already had a threat that if I call the police,I am a dead man!

It started happening at first in my own office cabin. She called me over the phone about some non – work issue and I ignored her; she came over to my cabin and just sat down on my lap, before I could say anything. She covered herself towards the wall and got my hands underneath hers . . . . Her previous husband got a divorce from her two – three years ago and she had a kid. She works there as apayroll clerk and supports her kid. She also has appos with some other people in the office who needed sex. She is also iriginally from India, came here through Pakistan, where she got married and then to Mexico – from where she crossed the border illegally to enter in U.S.A. Now she has a Green card and she has her apartment in the neighborhood where she brought me for her sex appeal to me.

I could not resist, as she arranged a van and a procession party, gathering all the office people who work there. If I could have run away, they could have shooted me right there; if I could have called police, they said they would put a 'Rape charge on me – as I am the guy'. They said they have all the money that they can spend to put the charge against me and police would work for them. The company owner sponsors for all these expenses gladly as he is older, is also a caucessian guy and can hardly tolerate me! . . . This woman of her fifties is named as Emma Silva and she has her neighbors supports at ther apartment.

We knew for sure that we are destroyed, but how to handle this nastiest situation in the life? We were so happily married and right now we are as any go – getters in America, facing the life threatening events where we needed some fair and friendly peoples support. Punam knew for sure that there is some Maffia concept in America and in Mexico and this filthy Emma Silva has her own gang to destroy her family of love. She tried to convince Bibi atleast to go to a doctor for a check up, which may not look unusual and then from there they could get the laws involved into the matter properly. But, Bibi falls down with the indication of such talks and shivers badly as if this is a fantom that he has to go through and Punam is getting that pressure on him! Punam waited fo rdays for Bibi to pick up the courage and hoped that the Maffia gang is not big enough, as Emma originally came from India – where there is no 'maffia'.

Bibi rested for a week under Punams home based care and then got a call from his work to pursue the work the next day – all the internal threats remained as is for him. Punam had no personal income on her to stand up differently than this situation. All her old friends and colleagues from the previous work are back in Romington, Texas who may have been some help, if they would. But all the connection are gone by this time after they were newly married and had their own private life and honeymoon since a year and half ago – where their usual friends gatherings they had regularly. Punam thought of what a mess she did by just leaving them aside and moving to a nice looking place! But there is no scope of repentence now, all they had to do is to manuvor through the situation quickly so that she could get her working status back and then could have a different source of income to tackle it. Punam could remember correctly the different pauses with her encounter to the nephew owner, Mr. Donald. His looks were so much unusual to go through when she went to pickup Bibi at the office reception. He also questioned her about her being happy in the marriage just a few days ago and she answered yes to all of such curious conversations to him. Right now it is just the opposite angle of situation where Bibi is Tortured sexually and it could get worse if they go to the local police and she has to make it right again!

The Office cabin

BIBI WENT TO the work after a week that the incedient has happened and Punam dropped him there and called him at work and the phone stopped with no answer and the same things happened. Punam could now pick up Bibi in the afternoon – but he is all filthy and fatigued and all tears in his eyes. They almost stopped eating their favorite foods anymore, they only positive things left for them was some deep prayer so that things could get better soon. Punam thought of – if the same thing should have ocurred to Punam, she could have been able to pull the trigger right then, with no dillema at all. But she is also a woman and being a man the situation in different in America, as Bibi has explained to her. He got frightened visibly with the depiction of their money power over to their little family. He also described how the man – eaters situation occurs at any U.S. jail when they just lock someone up before any judgement takes place. If you hae an attorney to fihgt for you, it is again the same question of money – who has the bigger amount of money, wins the case, no matter whose fault it is! Punam started hating America and being subbotaged like this in her dreamed of life! She wished that they could have been back to India, where she had all her previous establishments and such nasty things could hardly gets carried away! It is not th equestion of money but the morality and all – proof judicial system what cann't just abadon justice for moneyless people! God's mercy – what to undergo in American system. How big the Mafia system could be!!! Tears fall off her eyes for no other visible reason now . . .

The Immigration letter knocked at ther mail for the couple's interview after what she gets her Green card sanctioned here. It is all a very lenghthy process and this letter came to her after almost a year since they applied for it. Punam started fearing if the immigration officer would question about their marital life – which is so much destroyed with the unusual circumstances now!! She dropped Bibi off at the work the day before. Then again the same thing happened. Bibi is gone for that day, no answer over the phone and when she went to pick up Bibi, the same old fashioned reception with taunting statements. Now Punam realized the chain of reaction better; she cann't take the immigration interview without Bibi and that is why Bibi has been kidnapped. It is a meticulous planned action organized from bibi's office itself. All are involved to make the precise harassment for Punam to destroy all her astonishing status and establishment she had in her unmarried life! The Immigration lawyer for her is Mr. Rahman whom they selected from the yellow pages only and he is a getgo guy who does not support her at all except for the immigration paper work, filing. As determined, she just left a voice message for Mr. Rahman that for some reason, they would not be able to make it for the immigration interview by tomorrow – because it was such a short notice and they could not prepare themselves and Bibi got caught up with pending work assignments . . .

The Cavalry

R IGHT NOW IT is totally a fight to settle down in America with such a harsh – lengthy immigration process and the marriage is dwindling on a string at the moster's paws. She also made some research online to see what other alternative she could have to get back to her own feet. That Woman Emma also started to seize off their joint income from the joint bank account at Fargo – as she claims her share after torture!! Bibi is getting sicker and sicker unless there is a break. Laws do not bother about anything else as long as they have their steady jobs. Who could dare to argue after Mafia's paws, even at local laws!! Punam can also remember vividly that before she was married, she had another harassment by Tx local laws in with' Anomally pass' at work interview – where the police chief merely apologized with no restitution after the heart break; at that time she called for help the White house an the assistant of Gore, the vice president of America responded with some minor follow up at the local laws; nobody gives you any justice until you can fight it back with hiring good attorneys. There is no moral job that they perform as she used to have that back in India and that was just free of cost . . . .

She definitely does not have the money to save Bibi on this Mafia attack, which also came after her, her being happily married to Bibi. Emma, her new name, knew it for sure that when one hand gets perturbed, automatically the second hand suffers and that was her enjoyment of the life time. She could not have gained any physical access otherwise with her own indefinite looks and with having a clerical surviving job. She banked on her, breaking Punams merit and status to her aged, vague wheel. But now again it is the money that she should have to have a regular life back. Otherwise, she is lost in America where the immigration may or may not work anymore.

She ponders if it could have been easier for her to have her green card from the work itself where she were going to make $100K annual salary and benefits. she just thought of Bibi's sponsorship on her Green card is more solid than her employer's an she knew that the gap of her joblessness could only be a matter of couple of months instead of a year, as it is now. Bibi is eight – nine years younger to her and she dwindled in the thought of getting married to this younger gentleman unless Bibi should have urged so badly that he is good enough for her and in America the age does not matter in the old fashioned manner as it is a custom in India. But this torture pressure is living Punam out of shape for the first time in her life. She needed some rescue, some convincing force and rescue to save Bibi and her marriage in America.

The Cavalry2

S HE STARTED ATTENDING a local church in the neighborhood with or without bibi as is her situation. She tried to utter the torture out on Bibi to the local people, if they can be trusted over their Mafia influence and power. She also left an online note for FBI on the website, incase that works. She only heard back once from FBIs when they tried to make sure that Bibi came back by himself after the first missing episode. They did not scrutinize the matter if he was tortured or not and what marks he has on his body now!! Before Punam came to America on H1B, Punam read different articles and newspapers where they depict America as such a strong system where the crime can be tackled precisely. but her first experience with 'Anomaly pass' made her to believe the wrongfulness in the criminal justice system where people could hardly get help after laws done massacre. So in Bibi's case she could not dare to cross the line anywhere unless somebody else urges it out with her minor conversation of purpose! In her surprise, the church people offered some help with her stay in case, Bibi leaves her but, for certain it is not for both – especially for a married couple being. She also noticed that she, in her early – mid thirties could get some attention from the church but, Bibi in his twenty five years of age, being a Caucasian white guy does not catter any kind of sympathy from the church group people. Also that his parents are supportive to the job' work or torture as long as that produces money for Bibi. Punam left her hope for Bibis poor parents and would not talk to them anymore.

After a couple of months, Punam, being separated from Bibi filed for being a battered woman with U.S. immigration to keep her status alive and got a place in a condo of Mr. and Mrs. Muller in Orlando beach. She could see Bibi only three – four times a month only when Bib could come out from the Employers trap to get himself nursed and nourished from Punam. He does not know how long he could last with this extreme physical torture and hopes for the best to happen to both of them. He believes that Punam has some serenity power to save him and she only knows, how that could happen. Otherwise it is all her fault that she urged Bibi to leave Tx, his previous job and parents family. Punam scur of mind from the 'Anomaly pass' made her to leave Tx at once where she knew for certain the job for two Art designers of repute is hardly anything hard to find. In reality, jobs are hard to find in southern California, especially with any big company.

The Theodor

PUNAM FINALLY GOT back a limited time Work visa from U.S. Immigration, who is still processing her Green card on another ground of being a battered woman and it may again take a couple of years before she could finally have the Green card to have a stable work. Punam tries to find some piece from the Church and such gatherings and from the little meetings with Bibi where Bibi follows her instructions on everything – what to eat, what to wear, how to run away if the torture happens at stage1, at stage 2 and more; but in no way she could convince Bibi that he could always go to the local police and could show his marks of torture to them directly. He would shrink and go away as he explains the stage in the jail where all the inmates fight and fight like animals. He would certainly die there – as is the threatening that he is carrying away. For Punam's surprise nobody else offers a different job to Bibi and it seems that the 'Mafia threat' is for real. Also that she left another online message for FBIs with the depiction of Mr. Donald and Emma's attack onto Punams family – where they did nothing, no follow up at all!

Punam got another interview letter, this time for herself only with the U.S. immigration after she started working in some local odd job for a couple of months now. She got up in the morning where in her car she has all the prepared immigration documents by the yesterday evening and she confirmed it with her precious immigration lawyer, Mr. Rahman. He did not work on her case anymore as it came to a different ground of 'battered woman' rather than her previous ground of 'marital spousal' ground.

Another episode on it again . . . Somebody broke into her car before this morning at 7A.M. and stole all her properties, documents, immigration papers, educational certificates in original and her Indian passport and all the books she carried over to her. She again filed a report to the local police at Mullers city. They came, questioned, got finger prints and went out to processing. Punam had to call the U.S. immigration again to cancel and to request for rescheduling the interview as she already lost everything, unless recovered after burglary. She hardly could have the money to repair her car and get all the precious documents back – if that is possible at all. The church offered a little help to repair the car on Mr. and Mrs. muller's request – who acted very strangely on this accident. They had a dog in the condo, and it did not bark at all in the night time when possible the burglary occurred. And the eyes of Mr. Muller and of Mrs. Muller – who were in their seventies, though strought, were not straight any more. They hardly had anymore sympathy left for Punam. Punam realized that a tension got formed after Bibi came and visited her place at Mullers, where she started paying a rent of $400.00 after her odd jobs income. Bibi would always urge to stay in the same place at Punams but, they would offer no help for him straight. They would even ridicule Punam that Bibi and Punam both have their own incomes now, still Punam is battered and is staying on their mercy.

Punam decided to leave though she had no other doubt in her mind that Mullers committed the burglary on her and is trying to supply her precious documents to her old enemies probably, as they started acting up so instead of showing Godly mercy anymore. She made her mind up to find another work and place for her at first and got herself together after doing her laundry. Bibi joined her there, just to have tears on their separated properties and such livings instead of having the precious joint home and livings. Their joint home is gone out of hands as Bibi could not manage paying its mortgage where he had no money left except a couple of hundred dollars in the wallet as Emma took out all the money under the same or more vigorous threat to him. Punam suggested Bibi to move to his brother in Kentucky, probably – he could help him out there and try to leave his Rocker's work totally to come out of the uttermost vulgar situation what can even take his life, if prolonged further. This West California Business owners have money in millions at least to impose any probable threat to punams at any time. The local people are for the money, even if it is that bad money.

The Russavelt & Mafia

PUNAM MADE A good bye to Bibi when he finally left for his brother in Kentucky. She now took a little odd job for her as a cab driver, what she could do without having a house for her. She continued on it for a couple of months and proceeded with immigration process further who accepted her status and asked her to get a divorce formally that would help her immigration case. According to the U.S. immigration, you cannot be happily/ unhappily married and could expect to be granted a green card as a regular/battered woman. The regular status demanded joint interview and when that happens, Bibi is in the torture cell at Rockers, as scheduled!! Though the torture came upon them from Bibi's work at Rockers, it is something that the local laws have to prove and could proceed, rather than only Punam's alibi and document of bank statements and medical expenses and Bibis parents letter of support to Rocker's, torture for Punam. Local laws can't work unless Bibi, an adult can tell the whole story to laws by himself.

Bibi left california and went to his brother and after a couple of weeks found a new job a an art consultant with a local company in Kentucky. Punam survived through the rough stage by herself for the first time in her life. She writes to Bibi and Bibi promised to get her back as soon as possible after the immigration is settled. They also got a formal divorce as the battered woman status needs that, after their marriage was forcibly broken apart by Rocker's mafia.

Bibis brother could not take the pressure of Rockers mafia again as they, Emma started calling Bibi after discovering his brother's place in Kentucky. She had some investigator to help her out with Bibi's source as his new employer's record showed his Social security number to identify the payment that the business did. Rocker's money started controlling Punam and Bibi's destiny from there on. His parent already joined Rockers obligation and started getting some under – the desk payment on their sort of contribution to Rockers.

His Brother Mohi has sent Bibi back to his parents in Tx as Rockers offered a remote job offer to Bibi what he could perform from his parents in Tx. Emma started making moves to Tx and stayed at Bibis parents every week with a settled arrangement with Bibis parents. Punam was no good to them as they see who has the green card or not and which source can give them the money that they crunch for.

All the money Bibi would make from there, after paying rent to his parents house would go to the house – tank reservoir and his father got a gun to control over that money. Bibi asked Punam to come to his parents and to rescue him from the continual sexual torture by Emma as he does not know what else to do by himself and could die at any moment of time. Bibi knew that at this time Punam has some Green card status and could work and somehow could support Bibi so that he could get rid of this Torture job probably, if he could only survive further. Punam made herself to drive to Tx back in order to rescue Bibi and then it is another range of Kidnapping and money laundry and gun point threat to Punam for her own life and that they also got the local sheriffs to ask her to leave Bibi and the village or they could put her in a mental hospital or jail or she could get killed at any point, if stays around. Punam took a motel to stay and still could text to Bibi to meet her there and still could not make Bibi to drive off with her as Bibi has got a new threatening from Rockers that if Bibi tries to leave Rocker's at any point of time, he could be just killed – with possible no trace. Punam's alibi would be all thrown away when she would have that odd job income where hardly she could afford anything to support her testimony. Punam came to know for sure that Tx laws/ sheriff in that village are not just lying on threatening to her, they are commanding over her and her life could as well be on the stake. It is no mistake, it is real – the village level gun involved power game in America.

The Hope

PUNAM LEFT AFTER appeasing Bibi and giving him some idea of hope and came back to Austria in Tx where she thought of she could live by herself with or without having Bibi there. Austria is the metro and capital city in Tx. She got a job to provide artistic support for Molecule industry, a huge company on art dealings with multinational branches. She got this job from a local staffing place and she also got an apartment in Tx that would make her to stay at no distance rather than an hour from Bibi's place and Bibi must like that to have his support at Punams. Both had a couple of good months again where Bibi goes to his parents for a couple of days and stays with punam for the rest of the week. But Austria in Tx is no better than the village at his parents – Lobo. One day her car was taken away on repossession and she had been left with no car for her commuting. She hardly had savings to get another car after all this massacre has happened and Bibis money is all out of Punam's reach for over more than a year now. Punam decide to catch local public transport, which are almost as nasty to tolerate; but Punam had no better way to survive. Nobody helps unless you can have a good job and support. At this time, she again caught another problem from a local stalker who offered her some transportation help on one day and since the next day, demanded to have a dinner. When Punam refused, this fellow drove her to an abandoned airport and just strangled her throat. She started calling for 911 from her cell phone and he took that away; but, left her alone by making jokes and said that everything was nothing but some joke; she can go anywhere whatever and can have cell phone back. She has not to have dinner with him, if she hesitates, as she showed that in her behavior when calling for police!

She thanked God and ran to her new Apartment in Austria and made a phone call for Bibi. She made a phone call for Bibi and also reported that to the local police. The police came and made a report and asked her to keep the logs, if anything else happens. They did not arrest the man who is six feet tall and is very strongly built in his mid fifties or more. They also found him as a registered sex offender but still did not arrest him as there was no more evidence to support punam's alibi, as she took time to report it after taking care of herself. Some other local Austria people commented on their support for that man, Fadiv surprisingly, in the effort to put Punam Down after hearing her career stuffs. Punam knew it won't be easy for her to manage a life out here in Austria. Bibi came to her and tried to take care of Punam, as much. He would rather fight with this guy if he disturbs her anymore. He would also give his commuting car to Punam by hiding his parents. Punam got comfort from Bibi but, left everything else alone by remembering Bibis parents kidnapping episode of him from Punam after the same problem of Silva's from Rockers. Punam could not continue that work after some time as she received a threatening phone call from California newly elected Governor Mr. Edinger – who knew her established past and would comment on her jobs money now. Punam lost her apartment and got another

Days went by and Punam caught some Problem with her health with a fatal disease in a hidden shape in her – out of public mingling congestion. Now she has to care about herself a lot to survive in America. She hardly could manage to get a commuting car on her own when Bibi went vanished from her own apartment. Her stalker was continuing his function being off and on either by himself or by adopting some community guys from the neighborhood in Austria – where the illegal Muslim free living community guys were there apart from the black and Mexican and white guys with drugs and petty crimes. In fact it was totally an Agakhani community where she would get threatened if she would have visited a community convenience store. They would stalk her for sure to earn some petty money out of stealing/ vandalizing her specially when Bibi would have come for her and with some little money in hands to show his power being out of his mother. They must follow Bibi until they could strip him of money and then started the sex crime after chaining him once Emma could have established a chain from her California residence.

The Mafia Attack

YES, EMMA CONTINUED stalking on them both after doing the spying with money distributed investigators from the Rockers company. So Punam lost control previously on her Creditors, then on her job employers and even started getting stalkers problem from the lowly neighborhood. Though police had previously identified her main stalker, the registered sex offender, Fadiv – he is still on the loose and Punam faces him in the moments of her rush and poor hours, especially with the neighborhood disturbances. If she would report such ongoing activities to the local police, they would call for Bibis parents – showing their only posssible job part – who would indulge them to put off any report that Punam should have made. Punams divorce to Bibi made any claim on Bibis being attacked with his comming to Punams apartment got almost out of reach though they were still there together in the part of the week, even with all continual destructions from the neighborhood area of Austria.

Emma, in the mean time could connect her circle association to Punams stalker and even with anybody that Punam could get a phone call from. In Punams idea, she must have distributed more money to put the neighboring gang to stalking work at Punam and Bibi. So in Austria, Tx the gang was a lot heavier than that they had back in California

Finally that night came into reality where Bibi came home after losing all his money for about some three – four hundred bucks, that he could carry with him after avoiding his mother. He came home sexually beaten after being shackled on his arms to have another forced sex with a Bangladeshi Muslim Girl of the neighboring community under the supervision of the Monster,-Punam's stalker, sex offender,

Fadiv. Punam could not take it anymore and tried to convince Bibi immediately to go for a doctor's visit, he already carried all the yellow chain marks on his arms, which are bloody and deep. Bibi argued in the same way as before – do you want me to die or to live as long as we could have some hope for us. The ugly bitter money was the controlling chain of command – through the laws in Austria where the Tx governor's people would do any illegal business as long as that produces any money. And also that once Punam had visited the Governor's house as a visitor, after remembrance of Bibis early childhood visits there, she got entangled with some local laws alluring Ladywise reactions, what also contributed to her police reports being totally ignored and in fact turned down.

They sheered throughout the night hearing for any clumsy noise from outside, what could be just a knife flying through the window screens or a bullet that can shoot any one of them or all – in the house. There is no call for the police as they could make the same nonsense. They hung around each other until two o clock in the midnight when each one fell asleep in the heaven.

Punam woke up in the morning and Bibi was still asleep. Punam tried to take some picture of his recent wounds, but Bibi got up and made the same ferent urges on his life and status as before. They got coffee together and bibi took the medications as he gets after being beaten up for two – three years now. He does not have his I got anymore and every time he comes back weaker and weaker.

There is no furthering chance from there unless Punam could catch a break through. Punam decided to leave Austria and to move in some neighboring village, where the illegal gang can't follow them. Their stinging money level did not have much of a scope after all these neighboring harassment and tortures. Punam can't trust anyone anymore.

The Stalker Game

SO THEY DECIDED that Punam should get any place in the neighboring villages and would email/ text Bibi and Bibi could escape the neighboring gang to meet her there and could may have a totally fresh start in their couples lives. Punam got a paycheck by August the ninth and purchased an used car to make her move; she also texted Bibi about the village where she should be going by the same day evening – as Bibi could not live by himself without seeing her for more than two – three days with all these ugly bitterness and no peace. She checked her cell phone text and the emails – where there is no reply from Bibi. She frowned at herself and made herself to drive to the Dindy city village where she arranged a little room rent. Bibi was not there too as really Punam did not put that in the message. Her plan was to do that all just before Bibi comes there and when he calls her from near to her apartment in Austria. She knew that as usual all her emails and cell text messages were stalked by Emma appointed private or some distant laws investigators – who sometimes deleted some of her important, money carrying messages on jobs etc. America is so critically political beyond her precious life experiences.

This no sign of Bibi for more than a two – three hours gave her a clear omen signal and still she tried to concentrate on her own findings, before losing everything in life. No Clue, no response. She called police again ignoring the turn around obvious gestures. And they did so with filing a mere report and by ignoring her vicious stalker with all these carrying troubles on Bibi, as her life partner. They did not like her mentioning of Bib as her life partner, as they were prone to hear the Tx Governing lady talks, as visible as they could make.

Punam threw her tears through for the first time after all these bitterness and carry over's. Her life is totally finished. She has nothing else to hold on or to be proud of. This is what was waiting for her destiny in America. No Friends, no support – all are that do or Die defined . . .

She avoided any light even in the night and what else they could do to Punam – kill her separately or do that things? – It does not matter to her anymore that anything else happens to her now. She could have just died before Bibi, then she could have avoided all these cutting bitterness and sorrow in her deemed life. Why God did not indicate that before, even in the nightmares? . . . . She is just a lost and sabotaged woman who could be thrown off, for anything or for nothing in Austria.

She took a day off from her present work and then took another day off and got late for ten minutes on the third day, when she lost her job for being late . . . No friend, no care and got hardly some hundreds of dollars in her account left. She packed her belongings and just moved out of her apartment for searching for Bibi or his body out. God could at least give her that luck or strength!.

The Panic started cutting her off at first and she could not think of anything else rather than where is Bibi now? – Is he alive or dead already? She tried to talk to Bibi in her unawake mind; no response – it is all the dark that has spread around the sky – that signifies to nothing. She tried to see any miracle, any color that can tell her at least about the state Bibi is in. Austria police has reported that Bibi is missing is all her own statement and she did that previously at some four – five points – where nothing has been found and the detectives wrote a back note that she may be some EDP and if such occurring occurs again, there could be some intervention to take place. Punam remembers what have happened before. Bibi had been f'ked up before by mostly the same chain or another time by another chain of some Chili goup of illegal – legal petty gangs who robbed him off to earn their part of money while looted Punam social security and driver license cards, immigration cards to use the things illegally. Punam had some temporary stays in poorly neighborhoods where things happened straight away, irrespective of her systematic approach on rent and work with odd jobs, as available. She remembers one incident distinctly where the Chili group did the same thing to Bibi robbed him off as Bibi appeared to them wealthy and vulnerable. Bibi had to run off Emmas grasp to Punam to gather his peace, unless, he is dying! . . . .

The Shell Bomb

SUCH NASTY OCCURRENCES took place at Punam's rented shelter's nearby place and when Punam called police, they either intentionally or unintentionally arrived late or did no further digging into the matter to leave herself alone – as a part of her carrying out her life with Bibi, who is far less established than such Governor etc. who may had some sweet intension for her – as they behaed. They were not only limited to that, anything else that they could do, is to put a back stab in their report that she is dreaming of such bitter state where nothing has happened actually. In Chilis group case, after Punam could discover the hidden home of torture in that neighborhood, Punam phoned and texted to Bibi, when the gang got frightened and let Bibi to go away and Bibi just came out of that in the old fashioned bitter manner with high fever and physical trauma, hardly could walk up to Punam – standing in the outside.

Punam now remember everything in details and the reaction of calling police in such miserable cases. What else she could have done rather than making such police reports. In her own country, in India people won't dare to disturb her like these ugly, nasty attacks and could have been caught before that without any damage happened to Punam or to her family. Also that in India the political leaders are not on the top of the list to carry out their own intentions and infact they are pretty good and contended with their own families. In America, if some bad thing would happen once and you do not have the money to correct it, it would revive in the next cases – that wrongfully with their aggressive force. Punam sometimes think of that the force here work physically only, not intellectually; and before they think, they act – for what so ever the reason is. So the outcome is not always positive and assertive to make the system dependable. In Austria, it is hardly dependable and from now on she has to put through it – whether or not she could find Bibi out – as happened before with her intelligent persuasion and communication with Bibi.

The Monopoly Game

PUNAM FEELS THAT Austria police has ignored her case again, though at this time Bibi may have been killed for the final time, especially after the Monsters last attack! He did not communicate with Punam since when he was supposed to meet her. It may have been the same luck for him as was happening before – this time more aggressive and the end of life occurrence.

Nobody told Punam that America is such a nasty, sinful country where things can just happen like that and there may be any slight positive outcome of such occurrences; so the illegal and sinful people would dominate over her kind of nobility – that easily. It is also such a man-eating culture of food – eater relationship of survival – the food chain of Darwin. She could never imagine it before until she landed up here and experienced it in her marital life – for her life sake.

She tried to concentrate again. She can't live on what has happened before. This is another, more vigorous attacking episode that she has to manage besides the whole idiotic negligence of Austria laws. It is her own family and her own life only that she has to stand up, for sure. She believes in God and feels in some way to find out some clue into the matter. She has to just concentrate instead of crying. Her brain feels numb and vague and she falls asleep and wakes up in the next morning without any luck and had no food for three days. She vomited out the food particles she digested before and except coffee or tea, nothing else pleases her now. If she force herself to cook some little meal, she sees her hands gets numb and she feels motionless. She only tries to activate her brain power. There has to be a way out somewhere. She left her apartment finally after packing up her stuffs and put those in a storage and started driving around in the surrounding villages of Austria, after discovering them from the map.

She went to the first village that she circled in the maps and kept drying around all the streets in there, specially any bush, graveyard or any park. She remembers her attacker who got her to an abandoned airport for doing the physical harm or killing. She knows for sure that this Monster, as Bibi depicted him is capable of killing without any regret. He is six feet two and has big hands and feet, just like a Monster. Bibi told her before that the first time this Monster came across to Bibi when Bibi was rushing for Punam that desparately,a s he used to do and then this Monster came around to have some chit – chat with him before he can proceed for Punam. With that demand when Bibi went with him, probably he was watching for him before as the stalker had his circle in Punam's apartment and these people would be in the lookout for their hunt for Bibi. All her telephone, email, texting were sabotaged by some private investigator or black laws after Rockers broke out on her and her family Bibi. She can't request someone in power to stop it. Even somewhere in the laws they explained that if there is any hacking going on with her telephone and emails, even after she changed her passwords a few times – these are to protect her as she is a living delegate for them and that should not hurt her in any way. She could not argue further as this is the force and whatever they do that is all that she can take when there is no money to reerse or challenge anything. It worried her a lot but she came to know how to deal with it on an everyday basis.

Comming to her own life trauma, she tried to spot anything that could look suspicious. In her mind there is no other possibility than that – that is the Monster who attacked Bibi and he is either dead or alive; Hoping for the best, she feels it is not likely that they would kill Bibi and Bibi would forget Punam totally and would Die. He never surrendered to them to that extent unless he was totally bound by chains. In fact Punam kept pushing any suggestion of survival to bibi when he sees or feels the Monster anywhere. It improved his skill to run away from the attack and the attacker but, still did not minimize the scope of his being attacked, as everything is watched, every schedule, every move that they make – either on delegate obligation or on criminals politics as Mr. Donald of Rockers is a white Caucasian millionaire to deserve any harm over Punam and Bibi unless she has some stronger holds in U.S. system. Her surviving jobs are more or less nothing rather than supplying some little surviving money in the supply – chain management of man – eaters job circle.

As she analyzed her situation deeper, she felt a warm stab in her stomach and it tells her to run away from Austria and find out Bibi at any cost, without having the luxury of crying onto the fact; Bibi needs her for anything and for everything as long as he could linger to live. Bibi crunches on her for every perturbed instances throughout the time in their lives. There is absolutely nothing to change their partnership minds though, in the beginning Punam had doubts and confusions about holding out this relationship. It was such a big prestige issue for her to carry on this marriage. But, Bibi was that authentic to mean what he says and Punam tried to be better and better to realize and save her partner's life as he came across to all such ugliest situations just for her, being her partner only. Otherwise his life was fine at least before they met; he could at least have a professional industry job and routine to carry on without having such enemies. All became accessible to Punam's enemies is through herself only – as the center of point of destruction to their ugly fat egos with no skill, no reputation and nothing. This enmity got bigger for no other reason rather than the food – eaters happy beings concept. They are or were all that much zealous for her life and settlement, she could hardly imagine.

The Agony

IN HER MIND she never wished that bad for anyone, even for her bitter most enemy. She had her eyes on such issues but, if the chain and power gets bigger than that, she loses all the control that she had had before in India and early in U.S.A.

She knows from her own instincts that God won't betray her completely and there should be something somewhere that could be her help to find and rescue Bibi from the deadly trap. Punam laughed, if only he is still alive with all his charming agility on Punam!

She drove through the first village city from the list on her map – Digginger and no luck. She found some curious pillage eyes on her and ignored all and touched the interesting spots but, found nothing to hold on.

She know for certain that she has to try harder. There was not a single time when her own instincts betrayed her; she always had such a single minded communication organically with Bibi and that was all for certain. She knows that against all odds to her current situation, that is the strongest point that she has and she has the knowledge of the killing pattern form her stalker and for sure it is the same Monster that they were scared of in the night in the last bed time – which was merely a week ago to remember!

She stopped by in Culver city at a gas station where being away from Austria, no such video graphing camera to there to register her current image and minute details for the Agakhani retail chain to cope with. It's a fresh sense of relief for her for the first time after three years, being in Austria. She ordered a cup of coffee and tried to reorganize herself – without losing her smartness!

She knows still the village eyes would follow on her, as she is new to them and her looks are so different than theirs.

She tried to listen to any conversation from them that could be her subject of interest. Austria police said that Bibi went out from her on his own and will come back at any time if he wants, as happened before in their reports; so they did not file this under the title of 'missing person' rather with Punam's statement of the stalker, as she could think of, liable for Bibi's life incident – they titled it on 'stalking' merely without any follow-up in the direction; they made the indication of the stalker merely as an unknown person with the description of his physical measures and race and color and without a name to identify him – as occurred before in Austia police reporting.

They also indicated that Punam might find it helpful to hire some private investigator on her own to conduct such searches on Bibi, as she feels; they already checked out with Bibis parents who had recorded the same words and in the same tone that 'they know where Bibi is and he neither does want to see her nor that he has lost his life or faced any accident. All are casual and normal in there!' n Despite that all such bitter fat things happened to Bibi at every recent time of his visit to Punam, the records are all clear in the Austria police records and nobody is arrested or would be arrested as their intention is to clear all ugly patches out with no work!. They just work for the politicians and for the money handed influential gags like Donald! Punam or her own Delegateship is a minor case for them to work for unless there is any catch for their Governor's lady luck! They made everything very clear in their recorded statements and won't do anything further. She also called the state department, in case these different set of police should do something different being in the public safety, in general. They advised her the same to get a pirate investigator and incase she could find the body of Bibi, she could report that to the local police from where the work of rescue can begin on Punam's request. Punam thought of the idea of Bibi's body to find out – that means they know that he is dead already, and still they won't conduct any instigation!

She was comparing the attitude of Indian police force – how much pressure they get if something happens to some other countries citizens! That particular incident becomes their first priority on their governmental relationship whereas in U.S.A. it the last, just the opposite concept. Though she is now a green card resident or going to be, does not get any weight and in her worst time, they are asking to hire her own private investigators who claims a few thousands on retainer, before they could start the case even. The American agencies have no head ache to find out her life partner's life or death!! All they can do is their intended styling on showing some foreign delegating with wrongly formulated life concept for her. This is so abusive God, to imagine before! . . . .

The Hollow Barrel

SHE STILL HAS God to support her – this may be Christian God or something else. She went to some church gathering and services before who considered her like some adopted concept, even in sharing Gods love and sharing, as is the Christian custom. She knows for sure that in Tx, there is absolutely 'no help' luck left for her and she can't pursue any abdominal concept, as is her origin and strength. She sometimes feels that such kind of jerk got mixed up well with Emma's indented concept of separating them apart and kill them one – by – one after selling the bodies and skills. She had a very strong Devils brain to blue print such schemes over her. Her influence got bigger enough when Punam lived in Tx – which is so narrow and small in concept with some haggerdy set of earners livings – at least in Punam's surroundings.

Punam felt better after finishing up her coffee and got a fresh start on the engine and the car roared. Punam thought of positively on Bibis face and drove onto the next village city, Kotton village. Punam tried to find out if there is any renting house that they could have used to have Bibi – as they did before. There is none for some outsiders. So Punams thought went for Motels in the surroundings. None is there to rent with some cheap usage; but, there are some Bushy places around and who knows what was there in Bibis fate. Punam realized that some eyes were staring at her as some stranger. She thought of sitting down somewhere to observe anything suspicious on anyone. So found a crowded bar with village fellows having mugs of beer or woman in mid forties, mid fifties with wine glasses. No stranger as such that she could think of; they in fact gave some hug for Punam. Punam hesitated but took it as some common plate to stick to there for a while. Some more men and women, all single or dating partners came in and played some cards, videos and music's with high tone of voice. Nothing was strange for a while except herself where they were trying to crunch for on oldish, sluggish behavior. Punam had some little wine to finish as she is in a bar and of no surprise. People were talking and talking over the same or slightly different matters. Nobody was anyhow careful on anything except eating or drinking or dwendling.

St some point there came a woman in mid forties who recently became single and had some youth left on her. Guys were clinging around her precisely and she would carry on any and every sort of conversation with anyone. Punam caught her eyes and she started asking every detail out of Punam. Honestly, Punam could resist up to some certain ponts and when she began questioning her as well. She was a little more polished than the other people in there; though she looked like pretty lavish or open in behavior – what may match with the village culture. Somehow Punam noticed that she is trying to measure up Punam in a way that she felt something in common with someone there. Punam caught the flavor and started acting up in a way that she is liking her company and conversation. She revealed that Punam looked similar in at least cloths with some group of people who were there around a couple of nights ago; they drove to the bar at first and then possibly rented a motel and then they left. They were also from Austria.

Punam felt so strange in her inner being. She tried to carry the conversation pretty though she became numb in inside. She could not pretend herself any longer and a mixture of her tear and wine got mixed up in the glass she was holding out so carefully. The woman is Barbara and she seemed to have notice Punam and asked is there anything happened to her; she denied it politely and tried to get up and rush to see if there is anything up there that may have any sense with Bibis being. Punam can't remember anything further. It was not the reaction of wine. She sipped wine again and that gave her some courage and she tried to smile in ague and said – no, it's just the wine that made it like that, I am okay. The woman laughed a lot and carried on the conversation. She told her part of the life story and tried to hear the same from Punam. Punam choked and mimicked that she was separated as from Bibi and she does not have any kid, unlike that Barbara had a teen age daughter who is in school still now.

The Stalkers Peril

PUNAM SLOWLY STARTED asking her about whom she has seen before in the bar – that they came of Austria. Barbara remembered that there were a dating couple, somewhat odd looking and there was a Caucasian guy, young and timid, quite unusual there in the village bar. She asked her where they went, being like her neighbor. She looked kind of cautious all of a sudden and got up from her sit saying that I do not know anything more about them, they were just strangers came and drank and left quietly.

Punam got up as well and left the bar after saying good bye to her fellow bar mates. Once she started her engine, she broke into tears and she knew in her heart that it has to be Bibi with the couple, as Barbara described. Punam could not concentrate on the part of her role as a private investigator, as the situation demanded of her. Her personal feeling is more now than being practical. Part of her is roaring on the Monster couple as they took Bibi out of Punams holds and part of her is clenching for Bibi, at least one more time, where she can for sure fix up the situation and won't let Bibi go of. Just one more time God, one more chance in the life. Then the destiny may take its role and Punam won't complain anymore to anyone! Punam rubbed her eyes off and promised there has to be a fate for her and for Bibi. Bibi has to survive. No more strangling, no more hiding and seeking game. She can settle it down for certain, she is hundred percent positive . . .

After she broke her tears off, she finally started the car's engine and started driving slowly to the nearby surroundings, gasping every bit of inches of path. There are several village allies; one goes to a muddy hut. one goes to a bush; one goes to a river running through the village and there is one that goes to the broader street. Punam decided to check out the broader road at first, in case there is still some danger waiting for Punam herself, on any guess from them. Punam met with village fat dogs who burked at her car and ran around. Punam did not see any home nearby, may be that muddy hut is the house from where the dog appeared. In that case, here in the village, the dogs are buckle less. Does it make any sense for Bibis danger – the betterment side or the worsen side. She tried to think and feel deeply on Bibi and tried to find out if there is any message for Punam, as she usually gets on her cell phone or in email. She sees no sense from there. Certainly she knew Bibi was there a while ago, is he still there or he has again left with the Monster couple. She is making up this part from the description of Barbara and she won't lie about it, so obviously. Her stomach whirled and she felt a deep pain inside her. She thought of Bibi and Bibi in the last time has said 'I will go and come back in a day or two'; then Punam lingered it to a week or two until she gets her first pay check for the cars purchase. Bibi would become restless in the meantime enough to lose his own controls and this captivity must have occurred easily from there. Though Punam makes several plans for Bibi, not to get caught again and rehearses him on it, Bibi is good in it only when Punam is there around, even in his feelings; it does not work on him in distance, he gets totally blind and under control of the manipulative power as happened for a few years now!

Punam does not know if Bibi is alive or just a body! How to investigate her own partners being, being on the common string with all feelings and senses! The moment she makes herself smart, the next moment her feelings hold her back!

She prayed to God to get enough strength and wisdom to discover Bibis being, now at this earliest moment. Let God give her one more chance to tackle her partnering life, even over all obstructions.

She went to the broader way which is basically divergent from the highway and goes from one town to the next town in that belt. She drove straight in the opposite direction from where she drove in there. She noticed that there were seemingly three motels in that same town – Best Western, Town Lodge and Bicker Inn. As Barbara mentioned that they came in the bar for one or two days, she knew that there is a possibility that they stayed somewhere in that night. Barbara did not mention for sure that on the second day, the nice Caucasian guy was still there. It was unusual for her to have a nice looking Caucasian guy in that bar; so it was not anything surprising to her if that guy was absent in the next day bar meet. Punam justified the part of 'missing – Bibis missing', right here. If they could still be staying there, Bibi may have been bound by a shackle again or the worse is the worst fear in Punam that Punam do not want to know more now, unless needed.

Punam stopped by again in a gas station at the next light and got herself some coffee to remain alive in her nerves. She went to the motel Bikers Inn. The reception is shallow and difficult. The guy in the reception is the owner there. Punam asked if she can rent a room there for one night. The owner seemed to measure her up. She does not have any look similar to a Pros. She is kind of snobby for a villager; but, in her surprise the motel owner tried to look up on her, for any strange reason. She did not feel comfortable and so she asked again, can I please get a room here for one night? The motel owner seemed like stretching out his hands for money but is hesitant about renting to Punam. Is that the trio is still out there and she is carrying the same metro / upper class look? If that is the case, the owner would have come forward instead of being hesitant. That means there is some dirt in the business and it is not safe for Punam to stay out there. Punam said, she is feeling hungry and would come back may be after some time. Then the owner smiled in his ugly teeth and said okay to her. She drove further and found Best western motel which she cannot picture that the trio could have rented, as they were on bad trip altogether and won't to be caught. So Punam rented a room there at a nominal rate. The owner here is also from India and tried to accommodate her well in comfort. She felt safe there.

It was almost evening. she took a shower quickly and tried to eat something to fill her stomach. She could hardly eat in her bitterness and anxiety. So got up and hurried out to watch anything suspicious out at the other motel and drove around there carefully. She found a trail out there adjoining the river and there is a shop with different equipments for rent or purchase. She went there and tried to see if something could be of her interest. She had none to think of and so she was living when the owner of the shop came by and asked her what she was looking for. Smartly she answered a grass cutter or something just to relax around the river, that look calm and nice from some distance. The owner frowned but said nothing and Punam thought of investigating anything that is not natural. She started questioning about the different machines and the usage of those, as she is totally novice in that area. The owner looked like found some interest in describing his machines to Punam, whom otherwise the guys neglect and won't push know legible lectures like this. Punam thought of that is interesting. So on curiosity, she asked the price for purchasing or renting such equipments which are the Backhoe, mower, grass cutter axe and such things. The man answered that there was a trio who came by there a couple of days ago in the early morning, rented a Backheo for the whole day and then they returned the machine back in the afternoon before they left. The price was nineteen hundred dollars for only for the whole day. She asked what those people do with it. He answered that they came from a neighboring village and there they may have digged a well. In the village town, agriculture, planting, farming is common and a well can be used for anything. So Punam asked okay and left the shop on walking down the river way. some couples were busy in fishing and relaxing; so Punam mixed up well at the moment. In her surprise when she is searching the area around, she discovered a Blue jeans, torn off and a pair of socks that Bibi has; also she could match the part of the cloth from Bibis top that she purchased a few years ago from Wallgreen or Walmart. She panicked and tried to collect those in the back of her mind. The relaxing people were staring at her on her intentions. She basically left her sitting and walked around the river bank where she found a well, newly digged with some rocks placed on the top of it. She knew for sure the attack the Bibi faced and now it is the time to know if Bibi is alive or not. It is the question of Punams life as well.

The Center of the Earth Holdings

PUNAM WENT TO the well and started looking at the stones where some beer cans are scattering around. She also found debris from McDonald food and she knew that the Bangladeshi Muslim girl works there. Ignoring any curios eyes Punam collected the pices of Tee shirt and blue jeans – which were smelly after some rain fall. She packed those in a plastic bag and sat into the car before started crying on her own. She discovered a burial right now and Bibi is all gone by now. She could not hide her emotion any longer. People at the bank started asking her questions – what happened and she could not tell anything as these are all stories like nightmares and they may or may not believe her. She also did not know what they were up to and it is not easy to trust the village people as they already showed a different culture – each woman may or may not have a few men as boyfriends, even at ages.

She waited until it became dark and then tried to talk to Bibi – as she used to before and could get Bibi out of previous holdings traps. Fortunately it was a full moon night and when she became alone, she heard as if there is some heart breaking sobbing coming out of the gravely well; it is not her imagination but is the fact. She cried out in the sky – Bibi, Bibi – this is Punam right here. Are you there? She again experienced a sobbing coming out in a circle. Punam could not believe herself better and she knew deep down in her heart that it is real. Bibi never ever liked the concept of leaving Punam by herself and with Tx laws boasting, he would mention that If he should have been there in any such crazy scenario, he could do everything possible to stop them and then Punam could be fine. He knew any possible outcome, but he knew Punam a lot better than anything else and would not hesitate in such cases.

And also that they were trying to come out of the bitterness, Mafia attack in their lives. They tried hard enough to fight out of the situation and to rest on the earth itself, peacefully. Still it seems that the demonic power is more than ever and it circled through the people very well. Punam thought of dying right there, it is a-b-s-o-l-u-t-e-l-y T-o-o m-u-c-h to take. Her first reaction was to call police; but the strange eyes at the bank kind of stopped her at there for now and also that she is totally exhausted through the whole day and the buckles less dogs in there imposes another level of threat unless she has lights and stuffs with her to appease the situation!

She decided to leave the spot and to go back and rest in the motel, which is just a few blocks away. The only question remained if Bibi is still alive, her first reaction should have being calling for police and rescuing him out there right now. But her body can't take any more pressure. She has to settle down in herself to consume all such facts and details.

She went to her motel room, took a shower and fell asleep with no further notice of anything else. In the mid of the night, she got up on her bed and Bibis side is totally empty. She started crying peacefully by herself in the room. IS Bibi still alive there. She does not have any doubt about what happened to Bibi by now and she is not making up the things! All the people here are real and her brain is working just fine, as she justified her new situation. She is not a private investigator by herself, so such a life trauma, is all her new bitter most experience in life – they her life already broke in fractions – one by one, started a few years ago.

Her concept of calling for the police relies on the fact that police has to believe her in order for them to rescue Bibi. She also watched the strange fellow at the river bank, who were overly curious for Punam and would feel strange about the situation. Punam hesitated and waited until she got herself some hot coffee and some breakfast serial by herself, missing Bibi for the first time in her after marriage life. But she has to be more or less normal in order to tackle her case with the role of a private investigator, rather than being personal. She made herself to dire there again and as soon as possible with the sun rise. She for sure does not want to catch up with the Monster or even with the strangers – who seemingly felt nervous or uncomfortable to her. She tried to look at the clothes parts that she collected from the river bank. She could identify, justifying that these are all Bibis and even she remembers the occasion when she herself got those for Bibi. This is not a coincidence. It makes sense together. It is now the only question to let the police handle it correctly, Punam remembered Austria police and this village is adjacent to it, just in the country side. She is tossing on her weight verses all odds but, could not decide anything better than calling them. She also knew that according to the laws she needed to make the police report as soon as she realized Bibis missing and finding out his Body, may be in a grave.

The village Meadows

SHE KNEW THE indolent of the Muslim girl and that creates sense on having a grave – as Punam sees it. It is just made and some rocks are placed on the top of it and it rained after that. Bibis clothes and Eyeglasses are there with Punam – what else the instigators could look for! . . . .

She Came out of her bed and opened her door to watch the roadside, observing the sun rise in front of her. She went to the motel manager and started some conversation with him as he started asking her some personal stuffs. She can't imagine that she has to tell him that her husband is dead or with the possibility of being alive right there! . . . . She got some more coffee and waited to make some sensible conversation to put the topic out – to watch how he reacts to it. She could not do it well and everything comes to her personal life and what work she does and what money she has now. these are all village trends. So Punam prepared herself to go to the spot and take the challenge right away on her. She also went to a local Walgreen and got some vitamins one tablet for her and the rest she poured into her coffee cup and mixed and poured that down at the well, where the last stone was placed, seemingly that could be the position of his head. Punam remembered how they would share anything and everything and how she has to think of the best from this part.

The woman from the bar appeared at the spot strangely and smiled at Punam. Punam frowned inwardly and still asked her how she is. She replied that she is well and how is Punam. Punam said okay. She asked her why she is there early in the morning. She replied that just to be out there – that is all. Barbara also came to relax and probably do fishing. She had such fishing arrangements in her car's trunk.

She tried to offer help to Punam by suggesting to move with her in her apartment where she lives single and she thinks Punam needs some company as well. Punam agreed and moved with her to have some relief from the stretch. But she insisted that she may need to call police as she feels absolutely strongly that she has a situation with her partners life – a boyfriend in her words. She asked her to perform some Claudia work – an accurate tarot card reading to tell her fate about the situation. Punam decided not to proceed with that as they costs her per minute charge. Punam after a while called the police who came by and got the statement from Punam with some special village neighborhood talking with the woman. The woman works at a local restaurant and started living single after divorcing her husband who lives in the nearby village. Barbara plays a village prostitute, Punam realized and started seeing her boyfriends knocking at her door.

Punam though sticked to some detailed conversation about the incident to the police, who is a young officer of twenty eight years of age. He told her they have forty eight hours of response time. Punam after over hearing the conversation of him with Barbara, kind of doubted the accurate positive reaction that he should have taken.

Punam tried to find out any other resources out there. She found out a local newspaper name Bridge column she talked to the editor to publish a news store on her report as she felt something could go wrong even after reporting Bibis 'missing and 'body findings' in Kotton city. She can't explain the sound that came out in the hollow like Bibis urge of calling or such thing that filled out the hollow and the sky and it may have been common to anyone up there at the river bank. Beside that she detailed about everything else. And cried to request them to rescue him urgently.

The Upside is Down

S HE DID NOT know that she did some mistakes here. The police reporting may have been okay except that they were some force, out of the city culture. But the moment she reported it to the local newspaper, it became a challenge for them and on the next day when Punam visited the river bank to see what is the next effect, she found nothing else. She again poured down some bottles of vitamins into her coffee mug and poured it down the stones after locking at the spot minutely. She tried to pull out some of the stones but, they were extremely heavy for her to deal with. She visited the same mow shop on the roadway and asked the owner if she could borrow something to open a closed well.

He got at least curious and asked her where it is she replied that it is in the next village and the owner looked to trust her to sell his stuffs but, he asked to rent the Backhoe to dig out the stuffs from the filled well – which could cost $3000.00 a day. Punam tried to negotiate as her money in hands were much less than that and she now has no job to afford anything at all. She replied politely to negotiate on the pricing but, he was adamant and could not help her without the money at all.

The moment Punam again came back to the bank, there were police and sheriffs who at first looked like measuring her up and Punam politely asked what happened with her case. They told that they do not have the adequate resources to dig out the place on Punams findings. Also that they phoned Bibis parents who said that 'they found Bibi, he is well and healthy and does not want to meet her anymore and also added that Punam is a mental case as she did not have consistent work and house and such credit history – against taht Hr woman – Emma'.

Punams own statement that she is a reputed almost Art designer was just like a joke and they had no resources to estimate or verify her credentials in the village. Despite Punam had a work history in the same state in Denton city of Tx as working with Vilum – a big multinational art company as well in U.S.A., these local cops were too narrow for them to have such knowledge of the nature of work and that Punam, being an immigrant woman could hold this position in the Tx republican state! All added up to them as Punams imagination about herself and her Bibi being in this terrible condition.

The Cata-climax

PUNAM THOUGHT OF what a joke, Bibi does not want to see her and he is happy and healthy – so she has to rub out all the episodes from the beginning of the attack since years ago now and the situation near got better – especially Bibi was get visible weak and weaker everyday and he could hardly run, even being a marathon runner before. He is just thirty years old at this time but his life got so much tethered after the mafia attack. There was no escape. And right now the police is going to believe this lie from his parents who were deliberate to give him away to the mafia in order to earn money, when they themselves were not workable anymore and was living on social security money!

This police of Kotton said that they checked with the local authority over there which is Landburg Sheriffs who stood with Bibis parents alibi and there is no reason not to trust the local laws there. Also that that department is bigger than this Kotton police and sheriffs. Again they checked with Austria police where they found that Punam tried to report a stalking and the stalker is unknown in the report. Punam was so much surprised to hear such a non – reporting and Austria police just close all the reports out by minimizing their work – no matter if it is an accident, Robbery, sexual attack, death in this case after missing – but they won't care and close all the reports by putting some wrong title to it and describing wrong person into the report to lower the effect of crucial findings. Punam has hardly any money to challenge such vulgar laws. Laws are totally politically colored than being real. She feels how Austria police would show care for her lady-ish but would put her down slammed with the indication of Bibi and such episodes. She was fearing. If she should not have reported it, it would have gone against her as well.

She is now fearing. Also that Barbara when came to know the hollow sound and all that Punam has experienced, after finding out the spot, made her to tell the police that she doubts on Punams words and put her feminine zealousy into a money matter deal in case the police would still dig out the place and finds Bibi – alive or dead. Also that she lost her own husband on divorce she wanted Punam to lose hers as well. She is more aged than her, so she thought of having a better money status than Punam in Kotton village. Punam tried to stick around there as Bibi or his body – her partners being was there. She could not leave and had to come forward – no matter what.

Before the forty eight hours has elapsed, they came to Punam at the spot and asked her to go to a mental evaluation hospital in Austria for her own sake and they resisted any digging or rescue work for Bibi – what should have been the very first thing for them to do. They also recalled Bridge Column newspapers editors calling to them to justify the event – which came to them as a challenge from Punam and that part was true partially what Punam has adopted as a backup plan – so that she could at least push the things up.

They asked Punam to join the young cop in his police car to get to Austria mental hospital for an evaluation or they would arrest her as in forty eight hours, they already got a commissioner's signature of such warrant. She is vulnerable to herself or to anyone, unless being treated. They just liked her honesty, somehow.

Punam got shaked completely before leaving the spot and her car and tried to say to Bibi – not to worry and she should be back soon; Bibi had could help her out if Bibi is well. Bibi has a strong unique mental set what Punam never found in anyone else – even in herself. He could make the things happen with some high ended state of mind of him. In this way, he still took care of Punam in her bitterly abused state, being present in mind from distance. So Punam wished him luck as before and went for the cruelty in Austria mental hospital.

Before they brought her there, they left Punam in a room with high beamed light for the whole night; so when they drove to Austria, Punams eyes were swollen and different than usual, The hospital admitted her in without paying any attention to the fact that Punam lied in the same city before and she previously reported Bibis missing to Austria police – the hospital could at least make a check on that beside trusting this village cops. But they were deliberate to act equally for all – no matter from where the cops came in. Punam had no luck. They got all her physical exams done and nothing was different than usual. They had two three rounds of mental psychiatrists visit for Punam and she told them the same part of the happenings and requested them to take the action for real, who laughed at her and doubted about her degrees and further crucial relationships as Punam kind of told them about. There were only few attendants left who possibly believed her extremity and they tried to be cooperative to Punam. But it became a million dollars challenge in hands again in order to over ride all such odds and Punams helpless situation. Finally Punam met a public defender who took the case and got a date for a judge's trial. Punam was neat and clean and talked as little as she was instructed to and finally she got free and it is NOS – none unless found case.

Part of Lifeliness

S HE MANAGED TO get a taxi to come back to the same village in Kotton where her car was left and offered some more vitamin mixed coffee for Bibi after thanking God for this much even.

Punams life became crucial and it is only her pursuit to tackle this Mafia and other Governmental disturbances on her with the total polical catch. She could not feel safe in Kotton village by herself anymore and any mingling with the local pros – who looked sober from outside.

She though thanked her as she gave her the first clue after Punams own curiosity about the whole episode. The Kotton police never tried to justify who did what in Kotton, even after all this fresh signs and alibi of the related people. It was all a challenge of not pursuing or pursuing this case as the opposition came from Bibis parents village sheriffs at first. That got supported from another angle in Austria. The Mafia deal was there ongoing with no further resistance from anywhere. Punam never felt so powerless.

She started writing to the media and newspapers in the nation of America but, nobody responded her back. She contacted different private investigators on her own sake, they all demanded that big fat money, before taking the case. There was no luck and it was the Bush regime as well in Tx. She wrote emails to the white house and called them with the police and sherriffs conducts that she faced. There was no administration there and all they suggested is to hire private attorney for each case along with the private investigator. Her own meritorious records all getting slummed down to this level after all the works she herself could carry out. She is totally exhausted and frightened on the laws work here.

She still could not leave Bibi or Bibis body alone and took another silly job in the next city Falls and started living there after renting an apartment. The Agakhanis are odd out to reach there for her and she coudl probably take care of Bibi in the minimal way until she could at least save up three thousand dollars. She could not find any job related to her own professionalism there and she still started to find jobs in the nearby area from there that she could manage. Bibi is captive and is possibly alive. She has to just manage out her own situation besides the odds. America is not for anybody to live in – she experienced all that by now.

She has left some chunks of Indian money in her home country, she is missing all out here and she needs that so badly, so bitterly just to save her family's life. Nobody else seemed to be helpful, even with the lending of money. They also require the credit history, job status which are all so broke and poor after the mafia attack, including absurd laws.

The Bitter Slam

PUNAM WENT TO Austria and contacted the local FBI and the Homeland Security in TX – if they should take her case. In her surprise, they had all her testimony verified as these were and they were excited to plan for her with their internal who almost proposed to her when Punam is telling all ugly odds about the laws in respect of rescuing Bibi – starting from the Mafia after her green card processing and life in America. They would do nothing to any laws except Punam could have some second marriage is she should choose that. Punam refused politely and got angry with such sudden reactions totally in the opposite direction – what a culture!

Punam took different other jobs in the mean time – from the gas station job to, delivery job to Furniture sales but no Art job – which is her primary field. She got her green card after a short procedure at this time in Tx regional and now she has a Green card to exercise the laws properly, she thought. She asked for help even at the immigration office there to rescue Bibi, a sher immediate family, who were silent as she had a battered woman status and their after – living did not catter any strength for them to reconsider her request seriously. She found some jobs in Austria and again started facing the same trauma from the local Agakhani and such group leads. In fact, she got a car buglary on her car who took out about five hundred dollars of money – credit card combination when she was at a gym to keep her fit.

Austria police never arrested the burglar, even at this time and Punam has to decide how to take her cases.

It is all up to Punam to take the battle now. She planned to move to Denton agin where she had her professional job. In the mean time, the FBIs proceeded on picking up a girl in substitution for her for the FBI internal – the girl security form her gym who tried to support for the robber after destroying each visible pieces of information records on Punams car being burglarised there. It is that political patch, of supporting the crime and criminal involved upon Punams case!

The Casulty rises

PUNAM WAS SHAKEN but did nothing further unless she could rescue Bibi somehow to prove what is what, what happened to whom and all such curtail whereabouts.

The laws of crime and such crime supporter became completely abdominal in shape in Punams life. There is no 'direct financial support' – on these major life-accidents and wrongliness. People can just pass by with or without any emotion and that's it. It demanded all of her heavenly strength and courage to dig out the potential laws massacre.

The Austria based laws had another patch. They also crucially put Punam on an edged blackish ground – with comparison of crime's power over to Punam's singled handed sole in there. Punam would try to ask for help for rescuing Bibi, there laws would put Punam on a ban and punishment even – without any fear, under Bushism or Austria laws crime support! Punams prides are gone by now. It is merely the question of finding any justice. It is even hard to stand out, especially with the roofing being hit by the Crime gang! . . . .

They massacre all of her outstanding credits to demolishing furniture's – just by shouting at the creditors of Punam and by blocking, destroying her jobs as well as money savings. This is that big tremendous political crime influence! . . . .

Under her broken burglarized circumstances moved to the Dorn city, Texas – where she worked as an established art designer and people did know her there even before she was married to Bibi. She started getting some handful of raw traffic tickets by fallen laws there. They got so motivated to work on a bang socialism on her – with 'propose or be tortured' – the only two possible ground choices for her. There is no question of saving Bibis life, a valuable life – to Punam and, as well as being of valuable profession. Her poorly state after being Burglarized with all her identities being robbed of along with the credit card money, she would a creature by local laws and these are all her mistake on responsibility, being a regular driver of her own vehicle. Her normal regular life is their playing kite! She got being thrown to jail without any question of seeing a judge or seeing some frivolous judge in Tx – instead of seeking any fair justice system!!

The Proud pretance

THEY PRETEND, WHATEVER is abdominally wrong in anywhere, is good for Tx and it is their toohful agonizing pride that they are engaged to tear off the justice in their scope of own structured ruling system – with no fear, even with the matter of frauding the court papers with messing up the court documents. Even the FBI intelligence is engaged in such abnormal laws and would destroy Punam from any possible angle, by crossing any limit on her! The only count could be left of as being Sued by Punam and her positive support – it is that matter of God and Devil's literal existence and such battle. There is no promise that all the clean,fair things are fair in the justice system in Tx; it is basically just the opposite, in Punams cases.

Punam had to pursue on Bibis disappearance correctly and in any other fair system, otherwise she is involved into it – with not following the system. But in Tx system, it is her that they could disbelieve completely because of the traumatized looted appearance and leave the 'search & rescue' totally undone. Any stronger insisting or urge for rescuing her family's life becomes a compulsion and it even tried to put her in the other side of the law, destroying her nobility completely. By their offered, constitutional laws, she is supposed to have an A+ clearance and certifications offered by the U.S. Govt. instead they the Tx laws crime practice, offered her the ugliest survival for her – being the crime victim of such heinous crime, she is a blackly creature, not the regular criminals are; =the 'F' rate of her profile. They balance it with their pretense of smiley, casual face on her journey of 'Hiroshima – Nagasaki' laws handling. Her life and career is not anything important to them but her physical being is; they could do anything possible to let her – any such heads of laws, administrative heads. Nobody would care for her families loss of life and her being sabotaged completely.

The record shows hers being cleared of jail – her criminal background! There is no record of the killer – partners of her family did anything wrong. There is no record of completely wrong doings of the involved laws! They have the money to 'play joker with laws' and she did not have even the stand! They also put it in a democratic – republican phase with this 'Hiroshima – Nagasaki' persuasion. Any word for such mistreatment, could be even dangerous to utter, it is that Sadam Hussains laws and no part of fair justice system, as they boast of.

It is a cultural difference or something else, more intense and penetrating on Americas power propaganda! They make all these incidents pretty handy with some colored smile – where people could be fooled on the color and not on the basic morality of the laws.

If there is no constitutional practice, what could be the phase of the legal system!! Punam wonders at her life, her precious life in America! Is it the rudeness, that made America the most powerful country in the world or is it the blasphemy of laws that made it so big.

The Exempts

PUNAM USED TO know if some accident happens in life, people get around the victim, but if the manner that the accident has happen is due to the laws, who acted up totally unconstitutional – makes it a complete blunder for anyone to handle.

Only that God, being the heavenly father, embraces only the right doers and not the wrong doers at all – such a strong believe can for lawn in her inner smile while the outage of laws occurred on her in her regular being in the American society. Punam could embrace the God with no hesitation at all and that must give her the necessary strength of survival in the animal world of America – no matter if the American people of any race and culture would like it or not! . . . .

Her story ends in the Big O theory and her crying for a justice after her loosing of all – A+ character clearance of America. Bibis life and death is in the Devils hands and it is still not the time of God after seven valuable years of the American history.

www.ingramcontent.com/pod-product-compliance
Lightning Source LLC
Chambersburg PA
CBHW020353290526
45785CB00005B/2258